Learn to Play Bass with
Metallica

Left to Right: Kirk Hammett, James Hetfield, Lars Ulrich, Jason Newsted

Cover photos by Mark Leialoha (Jason Newsted) and Ross Halfin/IDOLS (Cliff Burton)
All quotes courtesy of *Guitar One* magazine

PLAYBACK+
Speed • Pitch • Balance • Loop

To access audio visit:
www.halleonard.com/mylibrary

4007-9026-3321-1455

ISBN 978-1-57560-333-9

HAL•LEONARD®

Visit Hal Leonard Online at
www.halleonard.com

Contact us:
Hal Leonard
7777 West Bluemound Road
Milwaukee, WI 53213
Email: info@halleonard.com

In Europe, contact:
Hal Leonard Europe Limited
42 Wigmore Street
Marylebone, London, W1U 2RN
Email: info@halleonardeurope.com

In Australia, contact:
Hal Leonard Australia Pty. Ltd.
4 Lentara Court
Cheltenham, Victoria, 3192 Australia
Email: info@halleonard.com.au

INTRODUCTION

Learn to Play Bass with Metallica is perhaps the most practical bass method you'll come across. Unlike other methods that teach you songs you haven't heard since nursery school, this book will have you playing cool music by Metallica right away, while teaching fundamental music topics such as rhythm, reading, and chords. You'll have so much fun that you won't even realize you're learning "important" stuff.

If you're a fan of Metallica, most of the music in this book will be familiar to you. If you're not familiar with Metallica—the most important hard rock group of the '80s and '90s—then this book will open up a whole new world of music for you to explore. This book will also leave you with the skills necessary to play bass in a band and kick some serious musical booty.

CONTENTS

C HAPTER 1

- •Introduction
- •Parts of the Bass
- •How to Hold the Bass
- •How to Tune the Bass
- •How to Read Tablature
- •How to Read Music

Introduction

This book is designed to be used without a teacher, so you can work at your own pace. Read through the text for each section, listen to the corresponding musical examples, and then try to play the examples yourself either alone or with the audio. If something is difficult for you to play, don't give up on it—just slow it down until you can master it and then gradually speed up your playing of the selection until it matches that of the audio. Don't skip over to the next section until you have mastered the previous one. Try to practice for a half an hour each day, but even if you can only clear a few minutes every day to play, you'll progress steadily in your technique and be kicking serious musical booty in no time.

Parts of the Bass

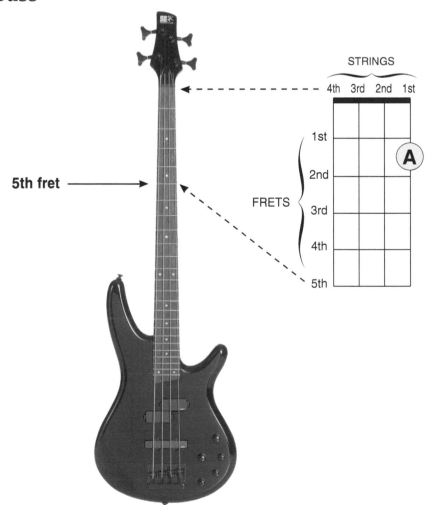

How to Hold the Bass

This book assumes that you are playing right-handed. If you are left-handed, mentally substitute "left" for "right" and vice-versa as you read this book. If you are sitting, rest the body of the bass on your right leg. If you are standing, make sure the bass is strapped securely and is at a comfortable height. Although being strapped low is *de rigueur* for rockers, it puts the left hand in an awkward position that makes playing difficult.

Sitting

Standing

The left hand is used to *fret* notes. You fret a note when you place a finger on a string between two frets on the neck of the bass. The thumb should be centered, behind the neck, with the fretting fingers, which are curved and with the knuckles bent, on the fretboard. Do not let the left-hand palm touch the back of the bass neck.

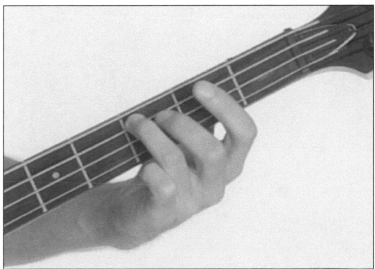

Left Hand Position (Front)

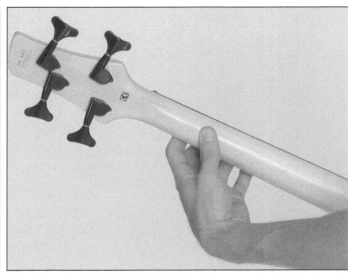

Left Hand Position (Back)

Using the thumb and index finger of your right hand, hold the pick with a loose, fist-like grip.

Pick in Right Hand

If you are going to use the right-hand fingers to strike the notes, rest your thumb on the pickup of your bass and pluck upwards, alternating between your index and middle fingers.

Right Hand Fingers

You can play one or more strings at a time by stroking them with the pick. When you play by strumming or plucking downwards with the pick, it is called a *downstroke*, whereas when you strum or pluck upwards, it is called an *upstroke*.

There are pros and cons both to using a pick and using your fingers. A pick will create a stronger sound, but fingerpicking generally allows for faster playing. These days, using the fingers is the more common technique.

How to Tune the Bass

Before you play anything on the bass, the first thing you have to do—and this is very important—is make sure the bass is in tune. Tuning your bass by ear is simple.

Conventional tuning of the bass is as follows. Note that the 4th string is towards the ceiling as you hold the bass and that it is the lowest-sounding string of the bass.

E	A	D	G
4th string	3rd string	2nd string	1st string

Track 1

Track 1 includes source pitches for all four notes, beginning on the 4th string and working up to the 1st. Tune each string by adjusting it until its pitch matches the corresponding pitch on the track.

A common way of tuning the bass is by using a fixed reference source such as a piano, pitch pipe, or tuning fork. To use a tuning fork, strike it against a hard surface and tune the 3rd string to its pitch (most tuning forks sound only one pitch—an A). Then, you can proceed to tune the rest of the strings using the 3rd string as a reference, as explained below.

You can tune a bass to itself when you have a pitch source for only one string (as in the case of a tuning fork) or no pitch source at all. When you do this, the strings are in tune in relation to each other.

To tune a bass to itself, use the 4th string as the initial pitch. If you're using a tuning fork, in step 1 make sure to tune the 4th string to the 3rd, not the 3rd to the 4th.

1. Play the note at the 5th fret of the 4th string and then the *open* (i.e., not fretted) 3rd string. Adjust the 3rd string accordingly until its pitch matches that of the 4th string.

2. Play the note at the 5th fret of the 3rd string and then the open 2nd string. Adjust the 2nd string accordingly until its pitch matches that of the 3rd string.

3. Play the note at the 5th fret of the 2nd string and then the open 1st string. Adjust the 1st string accordingly until its pitch matches that of the 2nd string.

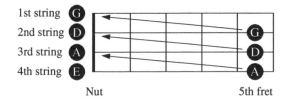

You may notice that there is a sort of pulsing or vibrating sound that occurs when you play a string. When you're tuning one string so that its pitch matches another, make sure that the pulses of both strings match.

One really quick way to get in tune is to use an electronic tuner, which can be bought inexpensively at most music stores. With an electronic tuner, you plug the bass into the machine, set it to the note of the string you wish to tune, play the string, and adjust the string until the machine indicates that it is in tune (follow the directions of your particular tuner). You should definitely know the old fashioned ways as well, but a tuner will come in handy when you're trying to tune in a loud environment, such as at a rehearsal or gig. A tuner will let you dive right into Metallica's music while you're still learning how to tune by ear.

How to Read Tablature

Tablature is to the bassists what Cliff Notes (no, not Cliff Burton) are to the student—immediate access to vital information without the prerequisite amount of preparatory work and study. Tablature graphically displays the string and fret location of any note, allowing bassists who are not fluent in standard notation, or who do not yet have a strong command of the fretboard, to find quickly specific note locations on the bass.

The tablature staff has four horizontal lines, corresponding to the bass's four strings. The bottom line represents the low E string and each subsequent line going up represents each higher string. The numbers on the lines tell you which fret to press on the particular string. A "0" indicates an open string.

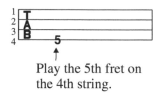

Play the 5th fret on
the 4th string.

The numbers are spaced according to where they fall (e.g., first note, second note, etc.) in the *measure* (the distance from one vertical line on the staff to the next—we'll explain this further in the next section). If more than one string has a number on it at any given time, then you should play all of the indicated notes simultaneously.

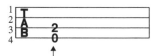

Play the 4th string open and the
3rd string, 2nd fret at the same time.

Although tablature is not intended to be a replacement for reading conventional music notation (explained below), it does provide one thing standard notation does not always include—an exact fingering for each note in a sequence. Since many notes on the bass can be played on more than one fret and string, tablature is used to offer the best practical fingering for a musical situation.

Warning: Music Theory Ahead!

What follows is a basic overview of the language of music. You don't need to speak the language in order to play the guitar. However, it's difficult to explain musical ideas without using the vocabulary of music. So you can skip right to Chapter 2 and start playing. But remember when you come upon a term you don't know, you can always come back here and look it up.

How to Read Music

The only person who was able to figure out time signature changes and write them down on paper was Cliff [Burton]. He had an immense knowledge of timings, musical harmonies and music theory in general.—Kirk Hammett

Being able to read standard music notation is very important for bass players. The concept of reading music has always been shrouded in mystery, but it doesn't have to be. The basics of reading are given here, while other hints are given at various points throughout the book. If you already know how to read music, you can skip the rest of this chapter and move on to Chapter 2.

The Music Alphabet

If reading music intimidates you, keep this in mind. While the alphabet has 26 letters, the music alphabet uses only seven different letter names: A B C D E F G. After G, the music alphabet starts over again at A. Only seven letters—how easy can it get!

How to Read Notes on a Staff

Music is written on a five-line grid called a *staff*. Notes are written on the lines and in the spaces between the lines. There are five lines and four spaces, and they are counted from the bottom up. For example, the lowest line is referred to as the first line.

A clef indicates a reference note for the staff. Most bass music uses the bass clef (also called the "F clef"), which curls around the F note on the fourth line of the staff. This tells us that any note written on this line is F, and from this note, we can find any other note by counting through the lines and spaces using the musical alphabet.

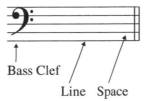

Bass Clef   Line   Space

The notes on the staff are organized alphabetically corresponding to the musical alphabet and in consecutive order of line-space-line, etc.

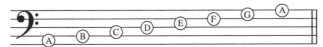

Notes on the staff are written from left to right, just like text, and are written across horizontally for melodies (notes played consecutively) and vertically for harmonies (notes played simultaneously). A bar line organizes the music into bars according to the time signature (we'll cover time signatures in the next section). A double barline indicates the end of a section or piece of music. Notice that bars are also called *measures*.

Bar (or Measure)

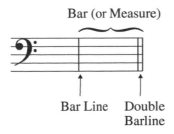

Bar Line   Double
Barline

Rhythmic Values of Notes

Here is a diagram of the most common note values.

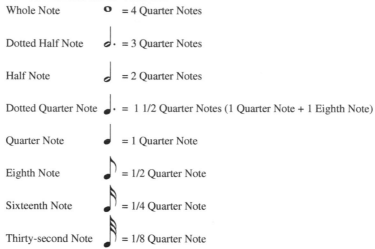

Whole Note	𝅝	= 4 Quarter Notes
Dotted Half Note	𝅗𝅥.	= 3 Quarter Notes
Half Note	𝅗𝅥	= 2 Quarter Notes
Dotted Quarter Note	♩.	= 1 1/2 Quarter Notes (1 Quarter Note + 1 Eighth Note)
Quarter Note	♩	= 1 Quarter Note
Eighth Note	♪	= 1/2 Quarter Note
Sixteenth Note	𝅘𝅥𝅯	= 1/4 Quarter Note
Thirty-second Note	𝅘𝅥𝅰	= 1/8 Quarter Note

Adding a dot to any notehead or rest increases its duration by one-half of its original value (e.g., a dotted quarter note is equal in duration to one and one-half quarter notes, or three eighth notes).

Rests are measured silences. Whereas noteheads and stems indicate the amount of time a note is held, rests indicate the amount of time that silence is present.

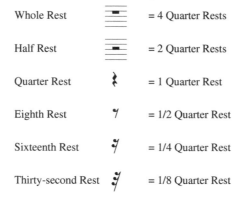

Whole Rest	𝄻	= 4 Quarter Rests
Half Rest	𝄼	= 2 Quarter Rests
Quarter Rest	𝄽	= 1 Quarter Rest
Eighth Rest	𝄾	= 1/2 Quarter Rest
Sixteenth Rest	𝄿	= 1/4 Quarter Rest
Thirty-second Rest	𝅀	= 1/8 Quarter Rest

At the beginning of every piece of music is a *time signature,* which looks like a fraction. The top number tells how each bar of music is divided (e.g., 4 means there are four beats in each bar), and the bottom number tells which type of note equals one beat (4 means a quarter note, 8 means an eighth note, etc.).

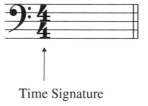

Time Signature

In each time signature, different beats are stressed more (or played more strongly) than others. For instance, in 4/4 the first and third beats are accented, and in 3/4 only the first beat is accented. Stressed beats are called *downbeats,* while unstressed beats are called *upbeats.*

Ties are curved lines that connect consecutive notes of the same pitch and combine their durations. For instance, if two quarter notes are tied, the result is equal to a half note. Only the first note of a tie is attacked, while the others are simply sustained for the combined duration of the tied notes.

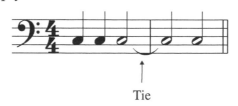

Tie

Half Steps, Whole Steps, and Accidentals

The distance from one fret to the next is called a *half step*. A two-fret distance is called a *whole step*.

Notice the half steps and whole steps in the music alphabet. The only half steps that occur in the music alphabet are between B and C, and E and F.

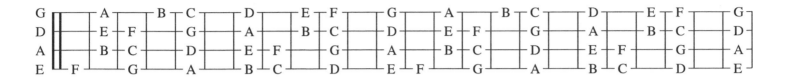

A *sharp* symbol (♯) raises a note one fret (or one half step), while a *flat* symbol (♭) lowers a note one fret (or one half step). For example, F is on the first fret of the high E string; F♯ is on the second fret. Sharps and flats apply for the duration of a bar. In other words, if you see a sharp before an F in a bar, any Fs on the same line of the staff that occur after it are sharp as well.

Any sharp note can be re-named as a flat and vice versa. A C♯ on the 4th fret of the 3rd string can also be called D♭, which is also on the 4th fret of that string. Sharps and flats can be canceled by a *natural sign* (♮), which also applies for an entire bar.

The notes of the music alphabet, in combination with *accidentals* (sharps and flats), make up a total of 12 different notes.

1	2	3	4	5	6	7	8	9	10	11	12
A	A♯/B♭	B	C	C♯/D♭	D	D♯/E♭	E	F	F♯/G♭	G	G♯/A♭

Here is the bass neck displayed with all the possible notes.

Key Signatures and Scales

A *key signature* appears at the beginning of each line of music and indicates which notes must be sharped or flatted; it also indicates the key or *scale* of the piece. Sharp and flat symbols appearing in a key signature affect all notes that are of the same letter (e.g., all Bs, all Cs, etc.). For instance, you may find a piece of music that contains a key signature with a sharp symbol on the fourth line of the staff. This means that each F throughout the entire piece must be sharped unless otherwise indicated.

A *scale* is a series of notes and is named according to the note on which it begins. For instance, a C scale begins on C, a G scale begins on G, etc. There are different types of scales, including *major*, *minor*, and *pentatonic* scales. You'll learn more about them in later chapters.

CHAPTER 2

- •The Role of the Bass Player
- •Reading and Counting Basic Rhythms
- •Shorthand Rhythmic Notation

The bass player's primary role in a band is to provide a foundation that is harmonically true to the melodic instruments (guitar, keyboard, voice, etc.), and rhythmically complementary to the drums.

While a bass part can be flashy and exciting, as Cliff Burton and Jason Newsted have repeatedly shown, it must never get in the way of the other instruments. Rather, a bass part should serve to enhance the music as a whole.

> *It's [about] maturing, and not worrying about playing so many notes. It's like if you're a bass player, play the bass.*— Jason Newsted

So, now we're gonna have some fun with the open E string, by playing some real Metallica riffs—but also work on reading and counting rhythms at the same time.

> Note: It is normal to experience some pain in your left hand's fingertips. After some practice, you'll develop calluses which will provide resistance against the metal strings that are now digging deep crevices into your flesh!

One of the duties of a bass player is to serve as an anchor of *tempo* (the speed and beat), keeping the band pumping along. To do this successfully you must have a good sense and understanding of rhythm. This example consists only of quarter notes; it may seem easy but the key is to keep the beat rock-steady, which may not be as easy as it seems.

Track 2

"Of Wolf and Man" Intro from *Metallica*

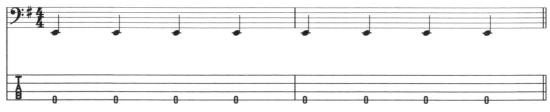

Words and Music by James Hetfield, Lars Ulrich and Kirk Hammett
Copyright © 1991 Creeping Death Music (ASCAP)

In these examples, be sure to *rest* (not play) on the appropriate beats.

Track 3

"Escape" Solo from *Ride the Lightning*

Words and Music by James Hetfield, Lars Ulrich and Kirk Hammett
Copyright © 1984 Creeping Death Music (ASCAP)

This example includes what's called a *pickup measure*. A pickup measure is an incomplete measure at the beginning of a piece. For instance, here you begin playing on beat 4 in that first measure.

Track 4

"Ride the Lightning" Intro from *Ride the Lightning*

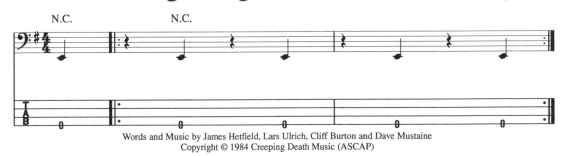

Words and Music by James Hetfield, Lars Ulrich, Cliff Burton and Dave Mustaine
Copyright © 1984 Creeping Death Music (ASCAP)

The "Ride the Lightning" example above includes repeat signs (‖: :‖) which indicate that the bars between the signs are to be repeated— in other words, played again. It's that simple!

CHAPTER 3

- • **Eighth Notes**
- • **Dotted Rhythms**
- • **Anticipations**

Eighth notes (♪♪♪♪ ♪♪♪♪) are counted in the following manner: say the beat number (1, 2, 3, or 4) for the *first* eighth of each beat, and the word "and" for the *second* eighth. For example:

1–and, 2–and, 3–and, 4–and, etc.

To help feel this rhythm, try verbalizing it using words that have two syllables, such as "pup-pet" or "sand-man." Compare and contrast this rhythm against a verbalized quarter note that has only one syllable, such as "one" or "lord."

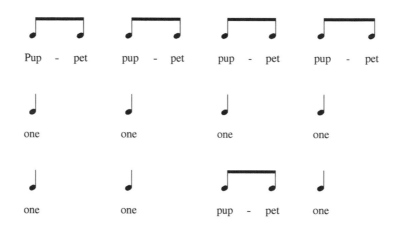

"Phantom Lord" Intro from *Kill 'Em All*

Words and Music by James Hetfield, Lars Ulrich and Dave Mustaine
Copyright © 1983 Creeping Death Music (ASCAP)

Here are some steady eighth notes. Pluck with alternate fingers (index and middle) or use *alternate picking* (picking with alternating downstrokes and upstrokes).

Track 6

"Enter Sandman" Intro from *Metallica*

Try this example which features a variety of eighth note/rest configurations.

Track 7

"The Struggle Within" Intro from *Metallica*

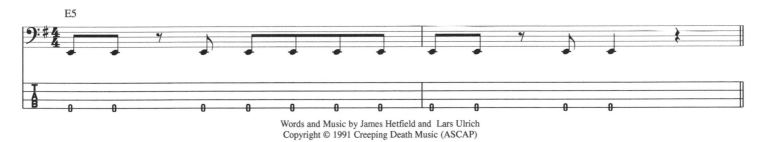

Did you have a hard time coming in with that third eighth note in the first bar? If so, verbalize a bar of eight consecutive eighth notes, but this time leave out the syllable on the first eighth note of beat 2. Do it verbally as many times as you need to and really try to hear it in your head before playing the example again.

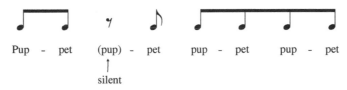

Here is an example with eigth notes including ties.

Track 8

"Sad but True" Intro from *Metallica*

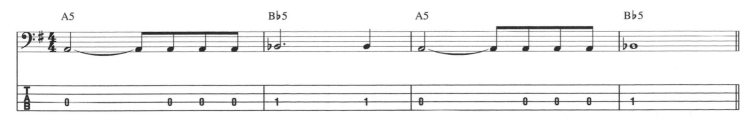

Single eighth notes are also commonly paired with dotted quarter notes. A dotted quarter note lasts for a beat and a half, the equivalent of a quarter plus an eighth, or three consecutive eighths. This rhythm is tricky to play accurately, so verbalize it and listen carefully to the accompanying audio. In addition to analyzing tricky rhythmic figures, it is also important to internalize the rhythm physically. Music is about using your ears and body, and being too technical can sometimes make things unnecessarily complicated.

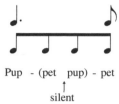

Pup - (pet pup) - pet
↑
silent

Track 9   ## "Enter Sandman" Pre-chorus from *Metallica*

Here's an example with dotted quarter notes preceded by eighth note rests.

Track 10   ## "Jump in the Fire" Intro from *Kill 'Em All*

In the "Enter Sandman" example, notice how the held F♯ in the second, third, and fourth bars falls on the upbeat of beat 4 rather than right on beat 1. This is called an *anticipation* because it comes in on an upbeat (earlier than expected) and is accented, creating the illusion of a shifted downbeat. Anticipations add rhythmic variation and vitality to music.

CHAPTER 4

- •Sixteenth Notes
- •Triplet Rhythms

Sixteenth notes are four notes evenly spaced across a single quarter note (which also means that two sixteenth notes take up the same "space" as one eighth note). They are commonly verbalized as follows: say the beat number for the first sixteenth note of a group, followed by "e–and–a" for the three remaining sixteenth notes. For example:

1–e–and–a   2–e–and–a   3–e–and–a   4–e–and–a

You can also verbalize sixteenths into a four syllable word like "Un-for-giv-en." To accurately execute sixteenth notes, use alternate picking.

Try to play the notes in this example as evenly and cleanly as you can. This example also makes for a great right hand warm-up exercise.

Track 11

"Damage, Inc." Solo from *Master of Puppets*

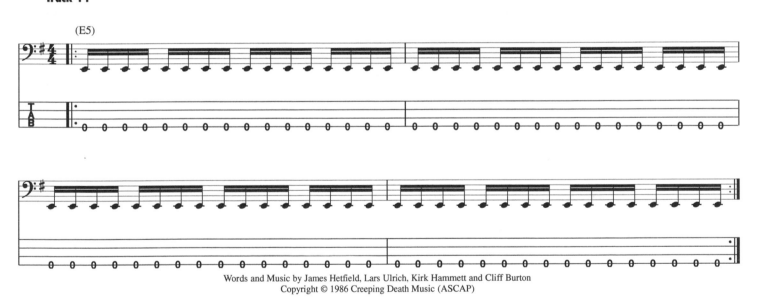

Now let's combine sixteenth notes with eighths.

Track 12

"Eye of the Beholder" Intro riff from ... *And Justice for All*

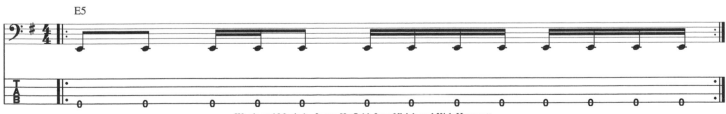

Triplets are groups of three notes normally played in the space of two and are commonly verbalized by saying the beat number for the first triplet note, followed by "and–a" for the two remaining notes. For example:

1–and–a 2–and–a 3–and–a 4–and–a

Triplets can also be verbalized into a three-syllable word like "bat-ter-y." To play them you can use either strict alternate picking or triplet picking (⊓∨⊓, ⊓∨⊓). Triplets can be very difficult to master when you are first learning to read and play. Listen carefully to the example to get a feel for triplets, and then try to play them yourself.

 Track 13

"For Whom the Bell Tolls" Intro from *Ride the Lightning*

 Track 14

"One" Solo from *... And Justice for All*

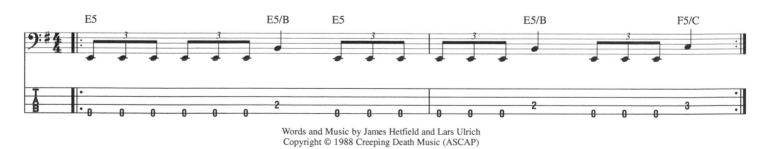

CHAPTER 5

• Reading Single Notes in Open Position

Now it's time to read music on the bass. Before you get scared off and sell your bass to the local pawn shop, keep in mind that this really isn't difficult once you get the hang of it!

We will begin by examining the notes in the *open position*, starting from the E string up to the G string. Open position uses open strings plus *first position* fingering. The index finger (referred to as your "1st finger") of your left hand frets all notes at the 1st fret, your middle finger ("2nd finger") frets all notes at the 2nd fret, your ring finger ("3rd finger") frets all notes at the 3rd fret, and your pinky ("4th finger") frets all notes at the 4th fret.

Here is a diagram of the *natural* notes (i.e., notes with no sharps or flats) in open position. Play through all the notes slowly, calling out the names of the notes as you do so, starting from the open E on the 4th string up to the B at the 4th fret of the 1st string. To finger the notes properly and efficiently, remember to use the open position fingering described above.

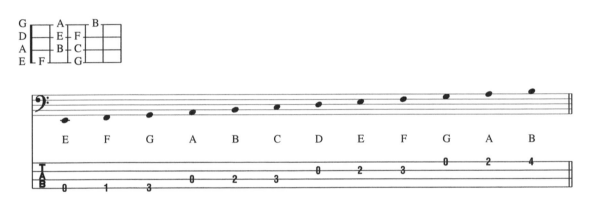

Let's work on reading some actual music now.

Track 15

"Leper Messiah" Interlude from *Master of Puppets*

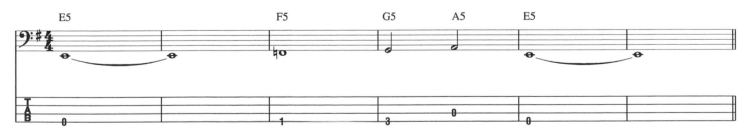

Words and Music by James Hetfield and Lars Ulrich
Copyright © 1986 Creeping Death Music (ASCAP)

This example includes an F#. Remember to use your middle finger to fret this.

"The Outlaw Torn" Outro from *Load*

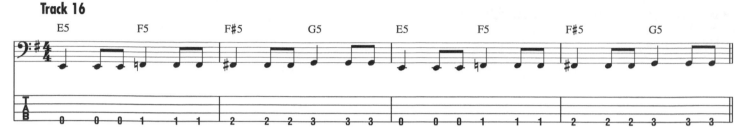

Words and Music by James Hetfield and Lars Ulrich
Copyright © 1996 Creeping Death Music (ASCAP)

Here are the same four notes from the last example (E, F, F#, and G) with some notes from the A string thrown in.

"For Whom the Bell Tolls" Intro from *Ride the Lightning*

Words and Music by James Hetfield, Lars Ulrich and Cliff Burton
Copyright © 1984 Creeping Death Music (ASCAP)

Use your pinky to fret the C# in this next example.

"Master of Puppets" Intro riff from *Master of Puppets*

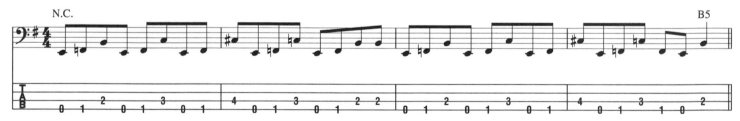

Words and Music by James Hetfield, Lars Ulrich, Kirk Hammett and Cliff Burton
Copyright © 1986 Creeping Death Music (ASCAP)

Here's a more advanced example that includes the 1st and 2nd strings.

"Wherever I May Roam" Intro riff from *Metallica*

Words and Music by James Hetfield and Lars Ulrich
Copyright © 1991 Creeping Death Music (ASCAP)

Try playing a few vocal lines on the bass to practice your new skills.

Track 20

"The Memory Remains" Bridge from *Reload*

Track 21

"One" Verse from ... *And Justice for All*

CHAPTER 6

•The E Pentatonic Minor and Blues Scales

I work with Lars when he does things, then I work with the guitars, and I still have to keep the bass going over here. So it's a very busy, riff-oriented type thing. I still have to keep the backbone and yet add accents.—Jason Newsted

Scales are a series of notes used as a resource for creating melodies and harmonies. Using the right scale for a given situation allows you to play or improvise in a key without hitting any "wrong" notes. The scales of choice for rock 'n' roll, past and present, are unquestionably the pentatonic minor and blues scales. These scales are the bases for countless riffs, licks, and runs.

Here are the patterns for the pentatonic minor and blues scales starting on E and based on open position fingering. Notice that the only difference between the two scales is the addition of one note in the blues scale.

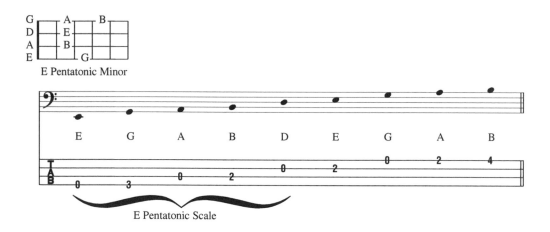

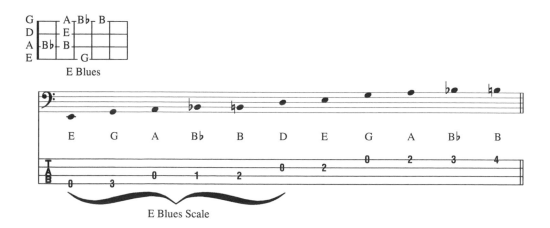

Let's try some riffs based on these scales. After playing through some of these examples, try creating your own riffs using these scales.

E pentatonic minor.

"Bad Seed" Solo from *Reload*

Words and Music by James Hetfield, Lars Ulrich and Kirk Hammett
Copyright © 1997 Creeping Death Music (ASCAP)

E blues.

"Enter Sandman" Intro riff from *Metallica*

Words and Music by James Hetfield, Lars Ulrich and Kirk Hammett
Copyright © 1991 Creeping Death Music (ASCAP)

"Sad but True" Intro riff from *Metallica*

Words and Music by James Hetfield and Lars Ulrich
Copyright © 1991 Creeping Death Music (ASCAP)

CHAPTER 7

- Bending
- Vibrato
- Slides

Now that your bass can talk, let's make it growl. The *articulation* of notes on the bass determines how the music comes across to the listener. Articulation refers to the way in which a note is played. Imagine two different people reciting the Declaration of Independence, with the first person speaking in a nervous, staccato (meaning that each sound is very short and defined, or "clipped"), rapid-fire, manner and the second person speaking in a monotonous, flowing, almost comatose drawl. While the passage is the same, the two people sound totally different because of their articulations. And it is their articulations that give them their identities. It's the same case in music.

On the bass, there are several expressive techniques that allow you to put your own unique stamp on anything you play. That's what it means to play *with feeling* or to have a *nice touch*.

Bending a note is pushing or pulling a string with the fretting hand to raise the pitch. When you bend a note, it is important that it is bent with a destination in mind. Your bend may sound out of tune if you go too far or not far enough. In music notation, the distance of a bend is measured in reference to a *whole step* (a two-fret distance, or the same difference as two notes two frets apart). For example, the fraction "1/2" next to a bend indicates a half step (or one fret) bend, while the number "1" indicates a whole step bend.

Here is an E pentatonic minor riff that uses bending.

Track 25

"No Remorse" Pre-chorus from *Kill 'Em All*

Words and Music by James Hetfield and Lars Ulrich
Copyright © 1983 Creeping Death Music (ASCAP)

Vibrato is an expressive technique that is similar to bending. Vibrato is the sound created by the rapid, continual bending and releasing of a note. This constant back-and-forth movement allows long notes to sustain and gives life to shorter notes. A vibrato is indicated with a wavy line.

A diagonal line indicates a slide. With a slide, you literally slide a fretting finger up or down on a string from one note to another. When you see a slide that has a starting note but no destination, slide your finger up or down just a few frets from the note, gradually releasing pressure, and then take it off the fretboard as usual in order to finger the next note. When you see a slide that has a destination but no starting note, pick a fret close by and quickly slide up to the note from there. You can slide more than one note at a time.

"Cure" Outro riff from *Load*

Track 26

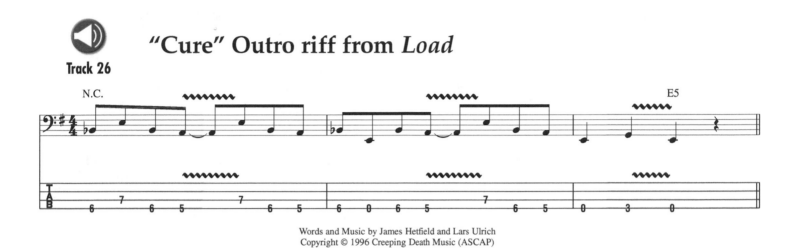

Words and Music by James Hetfield and Lars Ulrich
Copyright © 1996 Creeping Death Music (ASCAP)

CHAPTER 8

- •Hammer-Ons
- •Pull-Offs

Hammer-ons and pull-offs can be used to play two consecutive notes on the same string with a single right-hand stroke, and are good alternatives to striking every single note. A hammer-on is executed by fretting the note with a finger of the left hand, using the right hand to pluck the first note, and then using a different left-hand finger to strike (hammer) the second note higher on the string. Only the first note is struck.

A pull-off is executed by using a finger that is fretting the higher note to pluck the string as it leaves the fretboard. This plucking of the string causes the next note to sound, eliminating the need for the right hand to strike this second note. As in a hammer-on, only the first note (the highest on the string) is struck.

With an open-string pull-off, finger the first note with the left hand, pluck it with your right hand, and then pull your finger off the neck so that the open-string note sounds. With other pull-offs, place one left-hand finger on the fret of the first note and another on the second note; pluck the first note with the right hand and then remove the left-hand finger fretting that first note. As it leaves the string, it should pluck it, sounding the second note.

These examples use hammer-ons and pull-offs. If the curved line (also called a *slur*) connects a first note to a second note with a higher pitch, it is indicating a hammer-on. If the second note is lower in pitch than the first, it is a pull-off. If the notes are of the same pitch, it is neither—it is a tie.

You'll notice that a smoother, more "liquid" sound is achieved via hammer-ons and pull-offs.

Track 27

"No Remorse" Intro from *Kill 'Em All*

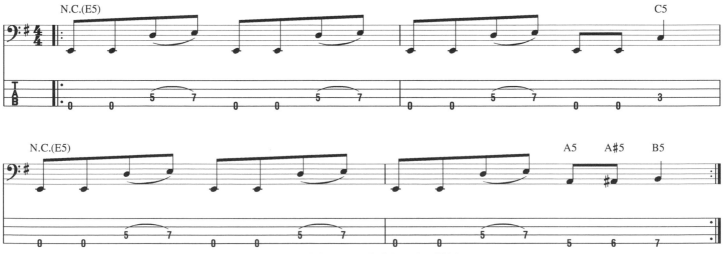

Words and Music by James Hetfield and Lars Ulrich
Copyright © 1983 Creeping Death Music (ASCAP)

Track 28

"Fuel" Intro riff from *Reload*

Words and Music by James Hetfield, Lars Ulrich and Kirk Hammett
Copyright © 1997 Creeping Death Music (ASCAP)

Track 29

"No Remorse" Intro from *Kill 'Em All*

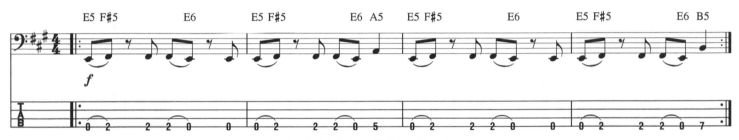

Words and Music by James Hetfield and Lars Ulrich
Copyright © 1983 Creeping Death Music (ASCAP)

C HAPTER 9

• **Reading in Second Position**

Reading in second position is similar to reading in open position. The only differences are that in second position, there are no open strings and fingerings begin at the 2nd fret.

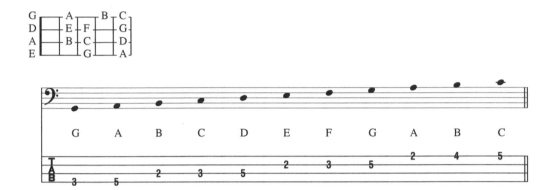

Here is an example from an earlier chapter, only now it should be played in second position.

"The Memory Remains" Bridge from *Reload*

Track 30

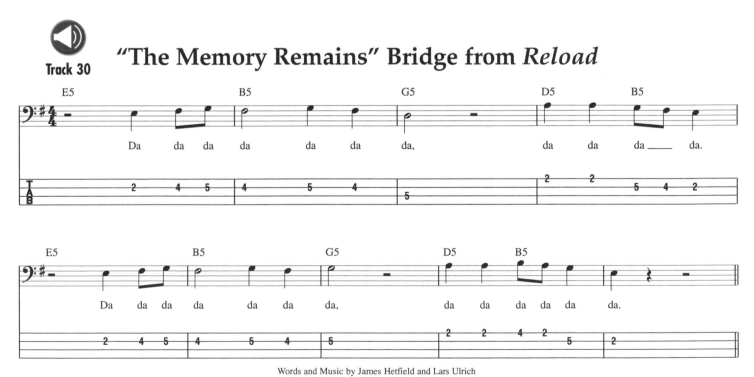

Words and Music by James Hetfield and Lars Ulrich
Copyright © 1997 Creeping Death Music (ASCAP)

Since open strings tend to have a more "ringing" sound than fretted ones, playing single-note passages exclusively with fretted notes provides a more uniform *timbre* (tone quality).

CHAPTER 10

• Moveable Pentatonic Minor
and Blues Scales

Pentatonic minor and blues scales are *moveable*—in other words, you can fret them in different places on the neck. Let's take the open position E pentatonic minor and blues scales and move them to a different key—say, G. Since the root is always on the 4th string, all we have to do is move the shapes up to the G at the 3rd fret of the 4th string.

Here are the finger patterns.

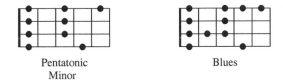

Pentatonic
Minor

Blues

Here is an F♯ pentatonic minor riff.

Track 30   ## "Prince Charming" Solo from *Reload*

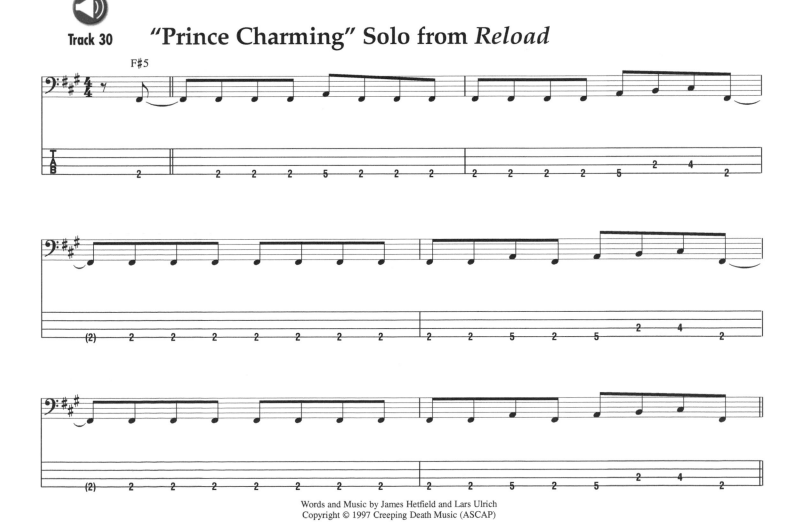

Words and Music by James Hetfield and Lars Ulrich
Copyright © 1997 Creeping Death Music (ASCAP)

And an F# blues scale lick.

Track 32

"Enter Sandman" Chorus from *Metallica*

Words and Music by James Hetfield, Lars Ulrich and Kirk Hammett
Copyright © 1991 Creeping Death Music (ASCAP)

Guitarists are masters of the pentatonic minor and blues scales, so why not learn from them? Here are some classic pentatonic minor and blues scales lead licks that are used by virtually every lead guitarist. Learn these licks and try to integrate them into your own playing. At first, it may sound awkward or contrived to just plop licks down in a "connect-the-dots" manner, but eventually they will become part of your musical vocabulary and flow naturally and spontaneously.

Track 33

"Jump in the Fire" Intro riff from *Kill 'Em All*

Words and Music by James Hetfield, Lars Ulrich and Dave Mustaine
Copyright © 1983 Creeping Death Music (ASCAP)

G pentatonic minor.

Track 34

"Jump in the Fire" Intro lick from *Kill 'Em All*

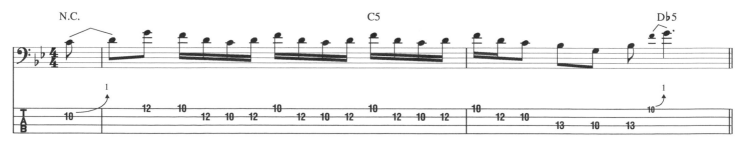

Words and Music by James Hetfield, Lars Ulrich and Dave Mustaine
Copyright © 1983 Creeping Death Music (ASCAP)

B pentatonic minor.

Track 35

"Fade to Black" Solo from *Ride the Lightning*

Words and Music by James Hetfield, Lars Ulrich, Cliff Burton and Kirk Hammett
Copyright © 1984 Creeping Death Music (ASCAP)

Track 36

"Orion" Solo from *Master of Puppets*

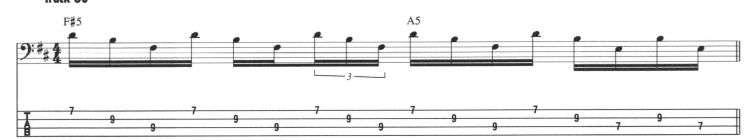

Words and Music by James Hetfield, Lars Ulrich and Cliff Burton
Copyright © 1986 Creeping Death Music (ASCAP)

CHAPTER 11

•Reading in Fifth Position

Here are the notes in fifth position. Your left-hand fingering begins on the 5th fret. The range is extended up to an E on the 9th fret of the G string—stretch your pinky over to fret it.

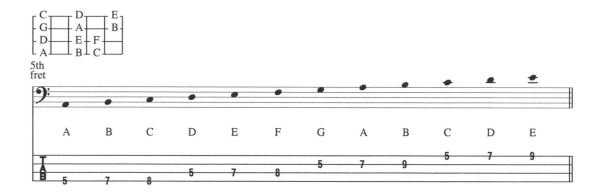

Let's see what our earlier open position and second position example looks like in fifth position. See how many different ways there are to play the same thing?

"The Memory Remains" Bridge from *Reload*

Track 37

Da   da   da   da   da   da   da,   da   da   da ____ da.

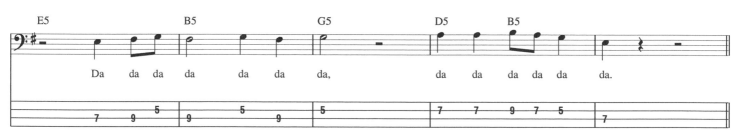

Da   da   da   da   da   da   da,   da   da   da   da   da   da.

Words and Music by James Hetfield and Lars Ulrich
Copyright © 1997 Creeping Death Music (ASCAP)

Let's do some more reading in fifth position.

Track 38

"Battery" Intro riff from *Master of Puppets*

Words and Music by James Hetfield and Lars Ulrich
Copyright © 1986 Creeping Death Music (ASCAP)

Track 39

"The Call of Ktulu" Bass solo from *Ride the Lightning*

Words and Music by James Hetfield, Lars Ulrich, Cliff Burton and Dave Mustaine
Copyright © 1984 Creeping Death Music (ASCAP)

Track 40

"Master of Puppets" Interlude riff from *Master of Puppets*

Words and Music by James Hetfield, Lars Ulrich, Kirk Hammett and Cliff Burton
Copyright © 1986 Creeping Death Music (ASCAP)

Track 41

"Fade to Black" Verse from *Ride the Lightning*

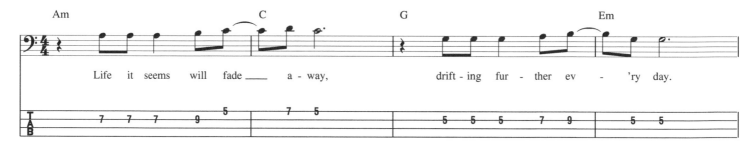

Life it seems will fade ____ a - way, drift - ing fur - ther ev - 'ry day.

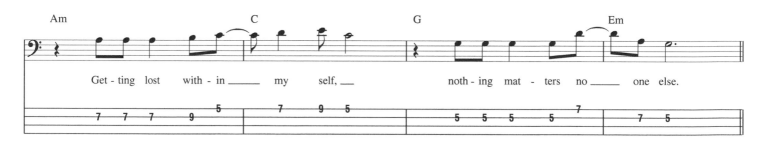

Get - ting lost with - in ____ my self, ____ noth - ing mat - ters no ____ one else.

Words and Music by James Hetfield, Lars Ulrich, Cliff Burton and Kirk Hammett
Copyright © 1984 Creeping Death Music (ASCAP)

This example has lots of *syncopation*, or accented upbeats that makes the piece sound rhythmically different than you would expect it to be in that time signature. To be the best, you have to master syncopation, so count carefully and don't let your sense of the beat get thrown off!

"Until It Sleeps" Verse from *Load*

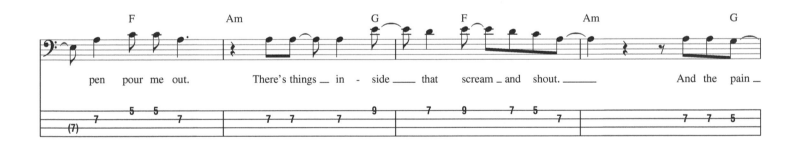

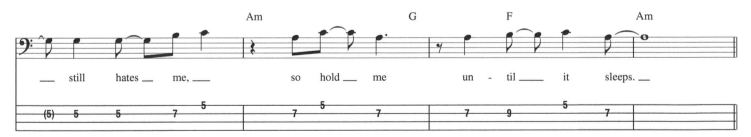

Words and Music by James Hetfield and Lars Ulrich
Copyright © 1996 Creeping Death Music (ASCAP)

CHAPTER 12

•Major and Minor Scales

Scales are series of notes used as resources for creating melodies and harmonies. The major and minor scales are two important scales to learn.

One good example of a major scale is the C major scale. It contains no accidentals (sharps or flats) and is made up of the notes C, D, E, F, G, A, B, and then starts over on the next C. Notice that there are whole steps (or two frets) between all notes except E and F (the 3rd and 4th degrees of the scale), as well as B and C (the 7th and 8th degrees), which are separated by one half step (or one fret) each. This arrangement of half and whole steps is what makes a scale major.

An easy minor scale to learn is the A minor scale. It also contains no accidentals and is made up of the notes A, B, C, D, E, F, G, and then starts over again on the next A. Here, there are whole steps between all notes except B and C (the 2nd and 3rd degrees of the scale), as well as E and F (the 5th and 6th degrees).

Here are three of the most common moveable patterns for several scales. Practice these patterns slowly, going up and down the scale until the fingerings are ingrained into your muscle memory. As you'll see as you progress, these patterns can be used in different parts of the neck to create major and minor scales.

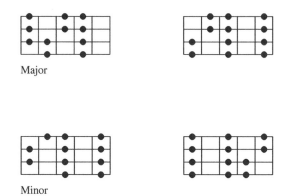

Major

Minor

Whereas the major and minor scales are more often used for generating lyrical, singable melodies and serve as foundations for creating harmony, the pentatonic minor and blues scales are used primarily to create riffs and licks, and otherwise improvise.

This example is based on an A major scale and climbs up this scale via eighth notes.

Track 43   ## "Hero of the Day" Verse from *Load*

Here are portions of the D major scale used melodically.

Track 44

"One" Pre-chorus from ... *And Justice for All*

Words and Music by James Hetfield and Lars Ulrich
Copyright © 1988 Creeping Death Music (ASCAP)

Here's an example based on the A minor scale.

Track 45

"Seek & Destroy" Interlude from *Kill 'Em All*

Words and Music by James Hetfield and Lars Ulrich
Copyright © 1983 Creeping Death Music (ASCAP)

This E minor example uses *left hand muting*, indicated by an "x", to create a choked, muted sound. This is accomplished by lightly placing fingers of the left hand on the strings while playing them. Listen to the example first to hear the effect and then try it yourself.

Track 46

"Welcome Home (Sanitarium)" Chorus from *Master of Puppets*

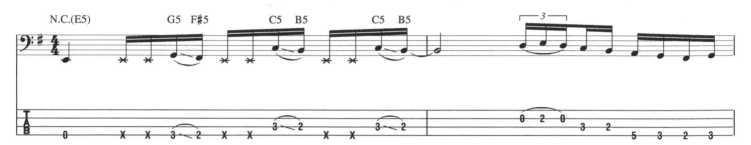

Words and Music by James Hetfield, Lars Ulrich and Kirk Hammett
Copyright © 1986 Creeping Death Music (ASCAP)

C HAPTER 13

•Reading in Seventh Position

Here are the notes in seventh position, a position that gives you good access to both high and low notes and is a good, overall position for playing melodies. Left-hand fingering begins at the 7th fret. It ranges up to an F on the 10th fret of the G string.

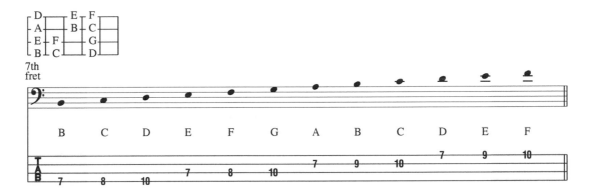

Let's see what our earlier open position, second position, and fifth position example looks like in seventh position.

"The Memory Remains" Bridge from *Reload*

Track 47

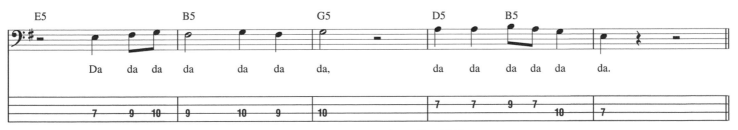

Here's some music for you to practice playing in seventh position. You'll want to get very good at playing in this position, as you will use it very often.

Track 48

"2x4" Verse from *Load*

Track 49

"Until It Sleeps" Intro from *Load*

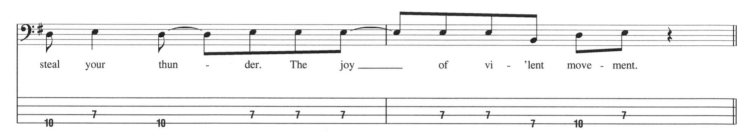

"Hero of the Day" Outro from *Load*

Track 50

Words and Music by James Hetfield, Lars Ulrich and Kirk Hammett
Copyright © 1996 Creeping Death Music (ASCAP)

"Fight Fire with Fire" Intro from *Ride the Lightning*

Track 51

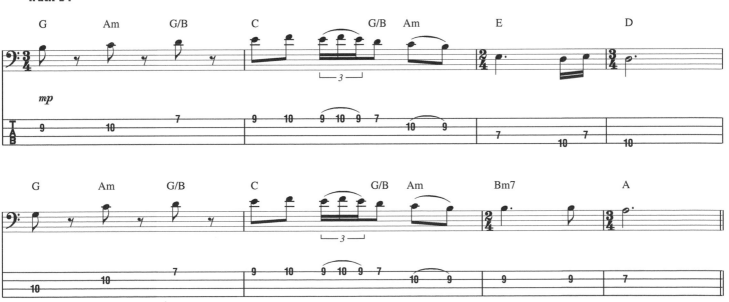

Words and Music by James Hetfield, Lars Ulrich and Cliff Burton
Copyright © 1984 Creeping Death Music (ASCAP)

"The Unforgiven" Intro from *Metallica*

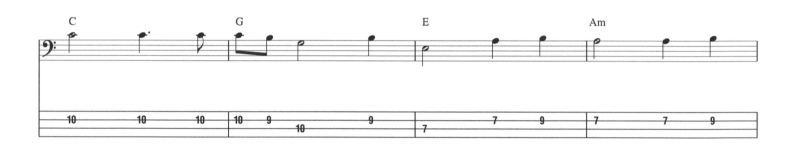

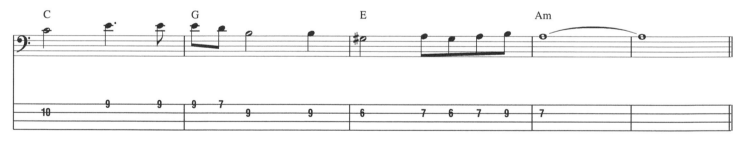

Words and Music by James Hetfield, Lars Ulrich and Kirk Hammett
Copyright © 1991 Creeping Death Music (ASCAP)

"Creeping Death" Bridge from *Ride the Lightning*

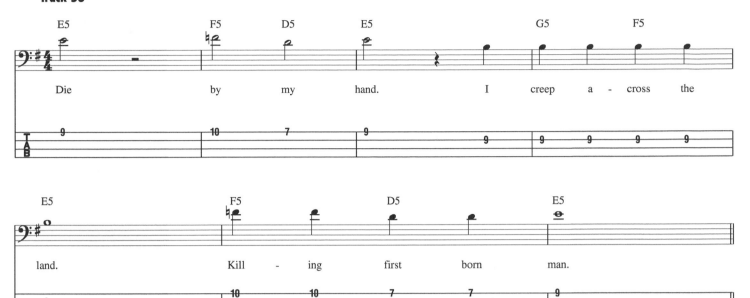

Words and Music by James Hetfield, Lars Ulrich, Cliff Burton and Kirk Hammett
Copyright © 1984 Creeping Death Music (ASCAP)

Track 54

"Mama Said" Verse from *Load*

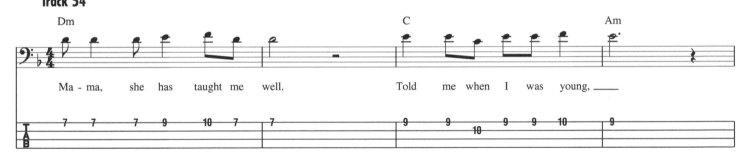

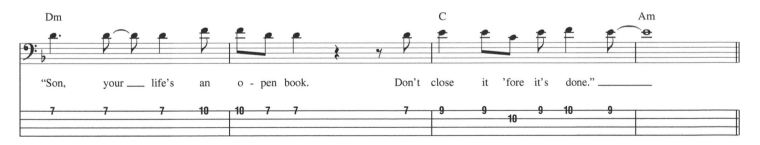

Words and Music by James Hetfield and Lars Ulrich
Copyright © 1996 Creeping Death Music (ASCAP)

C HAPTER 14

•Creating Your Own Bass Lines

The guitarist and the drummer write the songs. It's only natural they're the ones you can't compete with. You have to work with them.— Jason Newsted

So now that you've played all of those vicious Metallica's bass lines, you're probably dying to come up with your own. Let's face it, everyone wants their moment in the sun—and so do you! Just think of being on stage with all of the adoring fans and the flying intimate apparel coming your way, and think of the envy you'll instill in your friends!

Well, before you can make it big, you've gotta pay your dues. So, let's put in the practice time and check out some ways Metallica comes up with their bass lines so you can get some solid ideas of your own.

Here are some fundamental concepts used by Metallica and countless other groups for creating bass lines.

Playing Chord Roots

A bass player's first priority, no matter what style of music, is to lay down the *roots* (notes on which the chords are built or based). If the chord that is noted above the staff is an E chord, the root is an E, so play an E. If it's an E♭ chord, the root is an E♭, so play an E♭. Follow this simple strategy and you can't go wrong!

"Master of Puppets" Intro from *Master of Puppets*

Track 55

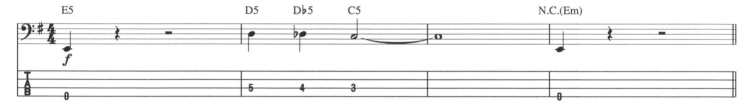

Words and Music by James Hetfield, Lars Ulrich, Kirk Hammett and Cliff Burton
Copyright © 1986 Creeping Death Music (ASCAP)

Adding Octaves

If you want to add some simple spice to the chord roots, try alternating between the root and its *octave*. The octave note is a note of the same letter but either higher or lower in pitch. For instance, here are two Fs.

One way to find the octave above a note is to count two frets higher and two strings higher from your original note.

Here's an example with octaves.

"Seek & Destroy" Solo from *Kill 'Em All*

Track 56

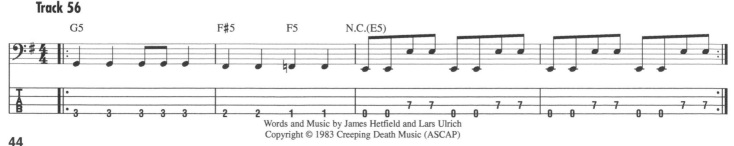

Words and Music by James Hetfield and Lars Ulrich
Copyright © 1983 Creeping Death Music (ASCAP)

Adding Fifths

5ths are another fool-proof way to go. A 5th is a note that is seven frets higher or six frets lower than a note. For instance, the 5th of a C is either the G above or the G below it. One good idea is to alternate 5ths between your roots and octaves.

Another way to find the 5th above a note is to count two frets higher and one string higher from your original note.

Fifth

 ### "One" Solo from ... *And Justice for All*

Track 57

Words and Music by James Hetfield and Lars Ulrich
Copyright © 1988 Creeping Death Music (ASCAP)

Adding Thirds

3rds determine whether a chord is major or minor, so some care may be needed here. Don't worry, though—once you get used to the concept, it'll be a piece of cake. A major 3rd is four frets above a note, while a minor 3rd is only three frets above.

If you are working with a major chord, you can use the major 3rd in addition to the root.

Another way to find the major 3rd above a note is to count one fret down and one string up from your original note.

Major 3rd

If the chord is minor, you can use the minor 3rd in addition to the root.

Minor 3rd

Another way to find the minor 3rd above a note is to count two frets down and one string up from your original note.

"Orion" Intro from *Master of Puppets*

Track 58

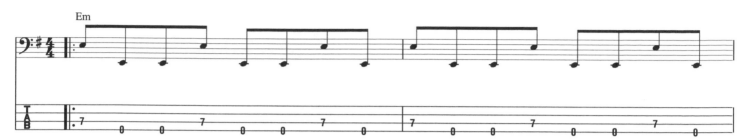

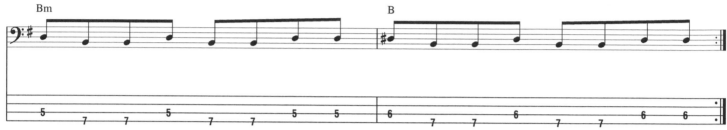

Words and Music by James Hetfield, Lars Ulrich and Cliff Burton
Copyright © 1986 Creeping Death Music (ASCAP)

Here's an example of a bass line that uses roots, octaves, 5ths, and 3rds. Can you identify them?

"Battery" Interlude from *Master of Puppets*

Track 59

Words and Music by James Hetfield and Lars Ulrich
Copyright © 1986 Creeping Death Music (ASCAP)

Using Scales

A scale is also an excellent source of notes for bass lines. Try finding scale notes that connect or *lead into* (or are right next to in the scale) chord tones (usually roots, octaves, 5ths, and 3rds). You can also just play chord tones on the downbeats and fool around with the notes of the scale between chord changes.

Here are two examples that use chord tones combined with some A minor tomfoolery.

"The Unforgiven" Intro from *Metallica*

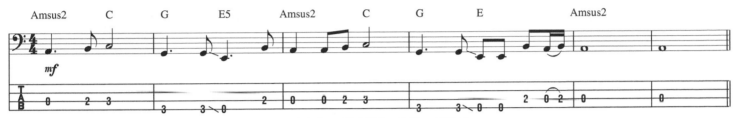

"Fade to Black" Verse from *Ride the Lightning*

Playing in Unison with the Guitar

Playing in *unison* with (playing exactly the same thing as) a guitar part is another option. Doing this thickens the texture and only adds to the evil.

Track 62

"Blackened" Intro riff from ... *And Justice for All*

Words and Music by James Hetfield, Lars Ulrich and Jason Newsted
Copyright © 1988 Creeping Death Music (ASCAP)

Track 63

"Seek & Destroy" Verse riff from *Kill 'Em All*

Words and Music by James Hetfield and Lars Ulrich
Copyright © 1983 Creeping Death Music (ASCAP)

Track 64

"Escape" Intro riff from *Ride the Lightning*

Words and Music by James Hetfield, Lars Ulrich and Kirk Hammett
Copyright © 1984 Creeping Death Music (ASCAP)

Now that you've mastered the music in *Learn to Play Bass with Metallica,* you're ready to take on more difficult pieces. You may want to try playing other bass lines from Metallica's music or that of other heavy metal groups, or you may wish to work through more advanced instructional books or collections of licks and riffs. You may even decide to take lessons! Whatever you do, you'll find that the techniques you've learned in this book will serve you well. Good luck!